STICKY LIVING

MAKE EVERY MOMENT MATTER AND LEAVE A
LEGACY

STICKY SERIES
BOOK 4

PETER LYLE DEHAAN

Sticky Living: Make Every Moment Matter and Leave a Legacy

Copyright © 2024 by Peter Lyle DeHaan.

Sticky Series, book 4.

Published by Rock Rooster Books

ISBN:

- 979-8-88809-089-3 (e-book)
- 979-8-88809-090-9 (paperback)
- 979-8-88809-091-6 (hardcover)
- 979-8-88809-092-3 (audiobook)

Credits:

- Developmental editor: Julie Harbison
- Copy editor: Robyn Mulder
- Cover design: Taryn Nergaard
- Author photo: Jordan Leigh Photography

The stories in this book are all true, as I remember them. I did, however, change some names and inconsequential details.

To all who see life as more than a vocation.

Series by Peter Lyle DeHaan

Sticky Series

In the Sticky Series of career development books, Peter Lyle DeHaan, PhD breaks down key business strategies in a coherent story-driven process to highlight what works and what doesn't. Through personal stories and eye-opening insights, he shares how readers can more effectively produce long-term results and increase their fulfillment.

Call Center Success Series

Join call center veteran Peter Lyle DeHaan, PhD as he shares a lifetime of industry experience to help readers operate their contact centers with increased effectiveness, produce greater success, and generate long-term profitability.

CONTENTS

STICKY LIVING

I n this series' first three books—*Sticky Customer Service*, *Sticky Sales and Marketing*, and *Sticky Leadership and Management*—we looked at life from a commercial perspective. The goal of these books is to produce business success and help readers advance in their careers. To make the work we do—and the results we produce—stick. To last and to make a difference.

Yet work only consumes about 25 percent of our lives (forty to forty-five hours out of a 168-hour week). What about the rest of our waking hours? Our non-work hours account for much more time each week. We must address this too.

In *Sticky Living* we'll take a holistic perspective, acknowledging that life is much more than work.

We must not lose sight of this. Work is not the end. It's the means to something better. This non-work time matters more; it matters *most*. It's family, and friends, and the connections that go beyond them, transcending vocation.

We want these relationships to be sticky. We want them to last. We want them to be significant. And this starts when we become sticky ourselves. It's when we live a life that sticks, one that lasts, that we can best impact others and live a fulfilling life.

May *Sticky Living* move us closer to achieving this important outcome.

Life Lesson

Let us be intentional about making every moment of our lives count.

FAMILY MATTERS

THOUGH WE CAN'T CHOOSE OUR FAMILY, WE CAN CHOOSE TO ENJOY THEM

My wife and I are fortunate.

We live close to our children and grandchildren. We had to move to make it happen, but it was certainly worth it. In case you're wondering, we first asked our kids for their approval before relocating. Though they cautiously accepted the idea at first, they later gave us a resounding "Yes!" and soon grew to embrace living near each other.

Now we all relish our proximity. It was a wise move and a cause for celebration.

Half of our family lives four miles south of us and the other half lives nine miles northeast. It's a quick drive in either direction. We see each half of our family frequently, sometimes weekly and occasionally more often.

On most Friday nights, everyone converges at our house for pizza. It's the highlight of my week. We share a meal and share life, enjoying each other's company, and the grandkids get to hang out with their cousins.

In this celebration of family, we have trivial conversations, and we have deep discussions. We enjoy being in each other's presence. I strive to have significant interaction with each family member. With intentional effort, this usually happens.

I'm better for it and hope they are too.

In doing so, I invest in future generations. It's a high calling as a parent, perhaps the highest.

Yet I realize this is a season in our lives. As our grandchildren grow, other activities and interests will pull them in different directions. Pizza with their grandparents may dim in comparison. But as long as this season lasts, I'll embrace it fully and seek to maximize its value and the impact I can have on my family.

I pray this season will last a long time, and that we'll continue to gather for Friday night pizza whenever possible.

This idea, however, didn't begin with my wife

and me. My parents started it decades earlier. We all gathered every Saturday evening for many years, starting when our children were young, continuing through their high school years and into college. Often, they'd invite friends to join us. And two of those friends became spouses.

The legacy lives on.

Questions to consider:

- What can you do to have a positive effect on your family?
- If you're estranged from your family, what can you do to repair the rift?
- If your family doesn't live nearby, how can you celebrate each other from afar? Alternately, what can you do to form family where you live?

Life Lesson

We will do well to seek to connect and maintain our relationships with family. Make family matter.

WATCH YOUR ATTITUDE
EMBRACE EACH DAY WITH INTENTION

O n a weekend trip, my wife and I found ourselves at a popular quick-serve restaurant for breakfast. "I'll have a number 10," I announced to the perky teenager at the counter. Her nametag said "Amber." She acknowledged my request and smiled pleasantly.

This encouraged me to make small talk while my wife contemplated her choices. Not fully awake, I said something apparently mildly humorous, causing our order-taker to laugh and brighten her smile. *What a pleasant way to start my day*, I thought.

My wife conceded that what she wanted wasn't part of a meal deal, nor were the items listed individually.

"Tell me what you want," Amber said, "and I'll see what I can do."

My wife listed three disparate items, and Amber began pushing buttons on her register. After a series of thoughtful keystrokes, she announced she had accomplished my wife's request. We paid for our meal and stepped aside to wait for it.

As the people behind us placed their orders, Amber's friendly demeanor continued to capture my attention. Suddenly, she spotted someone in her periphery. Her smile widened as she looked up. Her face beamed. "Good morning, Jimmy!"

In the split second it took for my glance to move from Amber to Jimmy, I pictured who I expected to see. Certainly, he would be her peer, perhaps a jock or maybe a prep, possibly even her boyfriend.

I was wrong. Jimmy was an older man with a weathered face, worn clothes, and a considerable limp. He moved forward with effort, alternating between a herky-jerky lunge and a short shuffle. After he made his way across the room, he didn't get in line. Instead, he headed straight to an open space at the counter near Amber.

With much effort, he produced a handful of coins, cupped in his twisted paw, and gave them a little shake. Two coins spilled out onto the counter and then a third. He poked his gnarled index finger into his open hand and moved it around as though stirring a pot. Then he flicked a fourth coin onto the counter, stirred some more, and released a fifth. With the last coin still rattling on the counter, Amber was there. She picked up the change, rang up an unspoken order, pulled a dime from the cash drawer, and carefully dropped it into Jimmy's still-cupped hand.

What happened next made me curious. Amber reached under the counter and pulled out two containers of cream and several packs of sugar. Then she turned to the coffeepot behind her and laid the additives on the counter.

Amber grabbed a coffee cup and filled it half full. Even more curious. Did Jimmy only want half a cup? She picked up one cream, gave it a brisk shake, meticulously opened it, and carefully emptied its contents into the cup. Then she repeated the procedure with the second cream.

Amber glanced up to see if anyone else needed her help. Assured that she wasn't neglecting another customer's need, she picked up a pack of sugar, shook its contents to the bottom and prudently tore off the top, pouring every granule into the coffee. She repeated this a second time, but then another customer diverted her attention from Jimmy's coffee for several moments.

She returned to the partial cup and added two more sugars. But her task was still not complete. Amber grabbed a stir stick and thoroughly mixed the contents. Satisfied with the results, she topped off the amalgamation with more coffee, put on a lid, and presented it to a grateful Jimmy.

She didn't do any of this begrudgingly or with indifference. She performed her task with all the precision of someone making their own cup of coffee. She was there to serve Jimmy, and she did so happily and without hesitation. Her kindness touched me. Such a gesture surely wasn't in the restaurant's efficiency manual, but it was the right thing to do. Amber's attitude established the framework for the rest of my day. If her example affected me so much, I can only guess what it did for Jimmy.

I imagine that when Jimmy woke up that morning, there was no question where he would go for coffee. His morning trek to the restaurant was likely routine. I suspect, however, that he wondered who would wait on him. He might have said to himself, "I hope Amber's working today. She treats me like I'm special. My whole day goes better when she gets me my coffee."

Likewise, I wonder what Amber thought before work that morning. Did she make an intentional decision to have a positive attitude, thereby producing a difference in the lives of those with whom she came into contact? She may have, but I suspect it wasn't necessary. I think her attitude of cheerfully going the extra mile was so much a part of her that it had become a habit.

While I focused on my own needs, Amber focused on those around her. And what a difference she made, not only for Jimmy and for me but for the other customers and her coworkers as well.

This challenged me. My attitude as I start each day affects how my day goes and has a ripple effect on those around me. Though it's unlikely I will ever match Amber's personable, outgoing disposition, I can aspire to her positive, helpful, serving attitude.

Life Lesson

Whether pouring coffee for someone or doing a more significant task, we can all be like Amber. It's not hard. All it takes is an intentional effort to have a positive attitude.

That positive attitude starts inside us, and it can start today.

CELEBRATE POSITIVE OUTCOMES
ATTITUDE MAKES THE DIFFERENCE

As a publisher of trade magazines, I travel to conventions and industry shows. Before that, as a consultant, I traveled to my clients' offices. Therefore, it may surprise you that I don't like to travel, especially to fly. It's impersonal and unpredictable, with minimal control over the outcome.

Yet, like any traveler, I have many stories to share.

A Private Flight

One time, awaiting a connecting flight and eager to return home, I sat at the sparsely occupied gate, immersed in my crossword puzzle. Suddenly, an announcement interrupted my focus. "Now boarding all rows, all passengers for Flight 3512. This is the final boarding."

That's odd, I mused. I'd apparently tuned out all the previous announcements.

Grateful I heard this one, I walked alone to the gate and handed the agent my ticket. "We wondered if you were here," she smiled.

Perplexed at such a strange comment, I smiled back and inanely replied, "Yes, I am here," and proceeded through the doorway. The door shut behind me.

After walking down the empty jetway, I stepped onto the plane. The flight attendant informed me that I was the only passenger. She asked if I would need beverage service. I thanked her and joked that she could take the night off.

When I deplaned, I asked if this happened very often.

"Occasionally," she replied. "Once the plane was empty. But we had to fly anyway, because it needed to be here for an early flight the next morning."

So, for the price of a commercial ticket, I had a private flight with a personal flight attendant.

The Captain's Final Flight

Another time, while anxiously waiting for the flight to my hub—where I would have a tight 40-minute layover—there was an announcement of a delay: thirty minutes, then an hour, then more. Finally, two hours past the scheduled departure, we had boarded and were ready to taxi.

Then the copilot made an unusual announcement. This was to be the captain's final flight for the airline, as he was retiring after twenty-two years of service. To celebrate, several members of his family were on the plane with him. As was tradition in these cases, we would taxi past two fire trucks, which would spray a canopy of water over and on the plane. As we proceeded parallel to the terminal, I noticed the windows lined with airline personnel waving their goodbyes.

Soon, passengers irrepressibly waved back.

Then came a surprise announcement: "Because this is the captain's final flight, ground control has given us priority clearance for departure. We are next in line for takeoff."

Never had I witnessed such a speedy departure. The runway even pointed us toward our destination.

In seemingly no time came another announcement: "We have enjoyed a strong tailwind and are getting ready to land. Because this is the captain's final flight, air traffic control has given us priority clearance to land."

Again, it was a straight shot to the runway, and we quickly landed.

Then came a fourth unexpected announcement: "Because this is our captain's final flight, ground control has given us priority to taxi to our gate."

Could it be? I wondered as I glanced at my watch. My connecting flight left on time—and I was on it!

Taking a Taxi Instead

For my final story, I traveled with two coworkers. Heading home, we landed at our connecting hub only to learn that our flight home, the last one of the day, was cancelled due to weather.

The savvier travelers snapped up all the rental cars, leaving us to seek other options. Alas, the only one was to spend the night there and fly home the next day. That was the last thing I wanted to do. I had anticipated sleeping in my own bed that night and anything else would be second rate.

Besides my preference, one of my associates was ill and anxious to get home. The other was beginning her vacation the next morning with an early flight out for a cruise. If we delayed until the next day, she would miss that flight and part of the cruise. There were no more flights, no buses, and no rental cars.

We were 150 miles from home. It was a desperate time. Outside, a city employee orchestrated cab rides. "What would be the possibility of getting a cabbie to take us to another state?" I asked. "We really need to get home tonight." My words dripped with desperation.

Seeing our weary faces, she responded positively. "Let me find you a good ride." After putting local fares in several cabs, a nice new ride with a competent-looking driver pulled up. "This is your cab," she smiled, with a grand wave toward our coach. She had a preliminary discussion with the bewildered cabbie.

Once I assured him I could provide directions, we were off. Four hours later, he dropped us off at our home airport. I paid the $380 cab fare, and we each headed home. Later, the airline refunded our unused tickets, so the net cost of our 150-mile cab ride was only $30.

Although there are other stories I could have shared —remember, I don't like to fly—I picked these three for a reason. Each one is positive: a private flight, a priority trip, and an accommodating cabbie.

These represent the perspective I attempt to adopt when I fly: be positive. Now apply this to every aspect of life.

Life Lesson

We need to be positive and look for the good in every situation. And there is always something good.

TIPS FOR SUCCESSFUL TRAVEL . . .
AND LIVING
A THREE-STEP PROCESS TO PRODUCE POSITIVE OUTCOMES

As I mentioned, I don't like to travel, with flying leading my list. Yet I have a strategy to best deal with air travel. It's a simple way to make the best of a situation I'd rather avoid.

Have a Plan

If I don't have a plan to occupy the idle time when I fly, I'll be bored and grow irritable. My plan starts with magazines to read. I don't take ones I want to keep, as each one gets thrown away after I finish it, making my load a little lighter. Magazines are for sitting at gates, standing in line, and before takeoff.

The crossword puzzles in the in-flight magazines occupy the actual flight. Movies are a welcome offering on longer trips. There is also the added benefit of the more objectionable material being edited out. Finally, there are the rewards I give myself at each hub airport: food. Frozen yogurt or popcorn are much-anticipated treats.

This plan beneficially fills my travel time.

Be Realistic

I used to have the expectation that an airline schedule was an accurate representation of what would happen. The fact that airlines began padding their schedules to boast a higher on-time arrival did little to erase my frequent disappointment. Then I realized a more reasonable attitude was to assume the plane would be late and to rejoice with an on-time or early arrival.

Here's why.

Let's say a trip has two flights there and two flights back. If one flight is late, do you remember the three that were on time? No. You dwell on the one that was late.

Now look at it mathematically. Assume each flight has an on-time arrival of 70 percent. That means that for the two flights to get to your destination, you only have a 49 percent chance both flights will be on time. To include your return flights, you only have a 24 percent chance of all *four* planes being on time. And if you have three flights (two hubs) in each direction, your odds of all *six* being on time drop to 11 percent.

By setting realistic expectations, we greatly reduce our chances of being disappointed. This isn't optimism versus pessimism; it's realism.

Make the Most of It

Is flying an activity to be endured or an experience to be relished? If your perspective is tolerance, you'll gravitate toward the negative. If your perspective is adventure (I'm not there yet), you'll remember the positive—like I did with my three airline stories.

Yet there are many more positive elements to embrace. You meet people you will probably never see again, yet a lasting impression can occur. A simple kindness to another traveler uplifts one's spirit. Even spending time checking out the airport architecture or infrastructure is not without its rewards.

Life Lesson

To realize a positive outcome, let's apply these three tips to every undertaking: have a plan, be realistic, and make the most of it.

GOING FROM GOOD TO BETTER

AN IMPROVEMENT MADE TODAY PAYS
DIVIDENDS EVERY DAY GOING FORWARD

I remember scanning my office years ago. The absurdity amused me. It contained an eclectic array of form and function. Although my computer technology was first-rate, the room's remaining accessories were a varied collection from different decades.

Of the six filing cabinets, three were metal and the rest were wood. With different finishes, colors, and styles, only two matched. The four shelving units were likewise dissimilar: early American dark oak, maple-adorned particleboard, light oak veneer, and modular plastic. It was not much to look at, but it all worked to my complete satisfaction.

My office, however, was not just about function, as it also contained a collection of sentimental artifacts: gifts from family and friends, trinkets from significant events, and a multitude of wall hangings —the most elegant of which was a tastefully matted and framed cover of my first issue as publisher of *Connections Magazine.*

Next to it was an evocative gift for my eleventh birthday, a reprint of an old-time sailing ship, bordered with a simple homemade frame. Then there was a 3D art rendering—the kind that you need to go slightly cross-eyed before the hidden image emerges. On the far wall was an avant-garde depiction of a Monopoly game in progress. The remaining item was a black-and-white photo, housed in an inexpensive, but seemingly ornate and likely antique, frame. It was an aerial photo of my grandfather's chicken farm, DeHaan Poultry, circa 1960.

That description remained fully accurate for over a decade, with my office configuration and contents serving me well. During that time, it underwent minimal changes. Even toward the end, it lacked little in terms of functionality, despite its diverse trappings.

So why did I want to ruin a good thing? Quite simply, I wanted to make things better.

I now had a work colleague: my wife. We set up

her office in a room on the main floor of our house. Mine was in the basement. It made no sense to have our offices on different floors, so I moved my office to the spare room next to my wife's office.

Although the upheaval of my comfortable office was borderline traumatic, the result has been worth it. An efficiency expert would deem my new configuration to be even better.

Moving also afforded the opportunity to simplify. I discarded several things and elevated others. I scrutinized files, streamlined my workflow, and reworked my computer configuration. Last, I bought a new desk and replaced my printer.

Moving my office required an investment of time and money. It also took a while before I felt comfortable in my new environment, but I'm better off having made the change. What I had before was good. What I have now is better.

Life Lesson

What changes have we been putting off in our workspaces? In our homes? In our lives?

Let's act now and enjoy the results.

LAW OF RECIPROCITY
RECEIVE, SHARE, AND GROW

T oo many people have a self-centered, protective attitude about knowledge. They want to receive information but are guarded about sharing it.

This is shortsighted. It is truly better to give than to receive. In this regard, I've developed a principle to guide me. I call it Peter's Law of Reciprocity. It states:

> Everyone you meet knows something you don't, so tactfully learn what it is. Conversely, everyone you meet doesn't know everything you do, so be willing to graciously share whatever you can when asked.

Over the years, this principle has served me well. When I have chosen only to receive information, my closed attitude effectively limited what I could receive. On the other extreme, when I opted to only share information, I grew to believe people needed what only I had to offer. This produced a patronizing attitude I hope to never repeat.

Receive

When seeking information, exercise discretion. Some things are off-limits, such as overly personal queries. Also, be genuinely interested in what you ask. Insincere questions short-circuit the free exchange of information. Quite simply, if you don't care about the answer, don't ask the question.

When you seek others for their opinions and ideas, it's acceptable to take notes. Don't rely on your memory. If you're like me, you already have too much to remember. Some people assume taking notes is rude to the person you're talking to. This is not so—provided you tell them what you are doing and why.

Just say, "This is important, and I want to get it right. Let me jot this down."

Making notes affirms the speaker and their

message. Note-taking conveys their ideas are note-worthy. You show respect by writing it.

Then repeat what you wrote. This makes sure you understood correctly, further honoring them in the process.

Share

Look for ways to share what you know with others. Be open to do so at every chance.

Here are some guiding principles for sharing information.

First, be careful not to betray a confidence or divulge a secret. It's critical to use discretion and common sense to protect and respect the privacy of others. If you don't, people will stop talking to you.

It's also important to not offer unsolicited advice. The only outcomes of giving unwanted counsel are people ignoring you or viewing you as arrogant.

Last, it's critical to not talk down to your inquirer. Instead, treat him or her as an equal.

Grow

It's human nature to talk to those we know. This implies that we tend to seek information from and share knowledge with our friends. There's nothing wrong with this, except that after a time, ideas— even bad ones—are recycled and then affirmed. When repeated often enough, people eventually accept them as fact, even if there's no reason to do so.

I call this *intellectual incest*, a provocative, yet apt, description of what happens with continually recirculated information among a small group of closely connected people. It could also be called an echo chamber.

Certainly, we should talk with our friends, but we need to be aware of blindly accepting what they say without weighing its merits.

When it comes to maximizing our learning, more valuable than interacting with our friends and acquaintances is interacting with those we don't know. These are the people most likely to share something fresh. This, however, is also much easier to suggest than do. Nevertheless, most of my *aha* moments have happened when talking with someone I just met.

If the goal is to learn and grow, then even more limiting than focusing our interactions on our friends is to restrict our attention to those we are with, be it family or coworkers. Although this is a natural tendency, it keeps us from hearing new ideas and diverging views.

When I traveled with coworkers to conventions or meetings, I often set prearranged limits on how much time we would spend together. This made it easier to interact with others outside our company. Yes, we planned strategic times to reconvene and share what we learned, as well as to just relax in each other's company, but for the most part, we intentionally split up, sitting with, eating with, and meeting with others. This maximized our exposure to new ideas and different perspectives.

Since it's much easier to connect with someone by him or herself versus when they're part of a group, this also makes us more available and approachable if someone wants to talk with us.

Though it's often uncomfortable to talk to a stranger or ask a question, that's when we receive the greatest reward. Similarly, it's when we freely share information that we unexpectedly receive the most benefit. Both instances lead to greater under-standing and enhanced perspectives, which is what interacting with others is all about—a mutual exchange of ideas and insights.

Life Lesson

Let's apply this idea of reciprocity everywhere we go and with everyone we meet.

SHOOT THE PUCK

TAKE INITIATIVE TO ACHIEVE THE OUTCOMES YOU DESIRE

W hen my son was young and began following hockey, I didn't share his enthusiasm. One day he invited me to watch the game with him. Inwardly I groaned, but outwardly I agreed, because that's what parents do. He made popcorn, and we plopped down in front of the television. I watched the play move back and forth, right to left and left to right. Soon the popcorn was gone, and my eyes wearied as one more journey up the ice began.

Suddenly, he jumped to his feet. "Watch!" The skater guided the puck past the blue line. It looked like the same play I'd already seen dozens of times. "They're going to score!"

The announcer's excited tone confirmed that

something monumental was about to occur. Play proceeded across the red line, then a pass and a slap shot, followed by total bedlam in the stands and an energetic high-five from my son.

On the second replay, I, too, saw the puck go in the net.

I stared at my son in disbelief. "How did you know?"

"Come on, Dad, you could tell it was going to happen as soon as he got the puck."

Obviously, there was more to this game than I realized. I began asking questions. For the first time in our relationship, our roles reversed. My son became the teacher.

He astonished me with how much he knew about the game and the subtleties he comprehended. With his help, my understanding of the sport grew, and my appreciation followed. Over time, I learned about a one-timer, the five-hole, power plays, a two-pad slide, and a poke check.

Soon, watching hockey became our favorite father-son activity. During one game, we watched an unproductive power play wind down.

"Shoot the puck," I implored the offense.

"They didn't have any good scoring opportunities," he said.

"But they can't score if they don't shoot."

My son flashed me a quick glance, followed by a brief look of comprehension before his attention returned to the game.

Perhaps I'd blurted something profound. After all, it made sense that if you don't take a shot, you can't score.

Regardless of the sport, playing it safe will not win many games. It certainly isn't the mindset of championship teams. How many times have we watched a team with a commanding lead squander it as they tried to protect what they had rather than build upon it?

The same applies to business. While extreme risk-taking is generally inadvisable, merely protecting your assets won't position you to capitalize on emerging opportunities. You could even squander what you have.

Even more important, the same applies to life. If you expect to coast through your time on this earth, hoping that everything will work out, you'll end up disappointed. Instead, take deliberate action to reach your potential and become the person you're capable of being.

I recall a poster that stated, "Behold the turtle;

he only makes progress when he sticks out his neck."

Whether it's hockey, business, or life, we can't score if we don't shoot.

Yes, many of our shots may miss the mark, but some will be on target. These will move us forward, propelling us to the next level.

Life Lesson

Let's take the shot.

OUR ACTIONS ARE NOTHING TO
SNEEZE ABOUT

WHAT WE DO INFLUENCES OTHERS

W hen my dad was alive, I realized that when I sneezed, I sounded just like him. Not that there was anything wrong with how he sneezed, but it was distinctive. At first, I chalked this up to heredity. But why did it take decades for me to realize the similarity?

I later realized other traits I shared with him too. I concluded these were not as much a byproduct of genes but more so of environment. Succinctly, as I spent time with my dad, I became more like him.

Beyond this physical idiosyncrasy, I learned more valuable characteristics from Dad over the years. A strong work ethic is a prime example. Dad never told me to work hard, he merely did so, and I copied his example. Other traits include integrity, honesty, and deliberate decision-making.

If I subconsciously learned things by being around my dad, what sort of things do people pick up from me? While I hope they absorb positive traits, I worry they could mimic some of my less-admirable tendencies.

Therefore, when someone close to us acts in a less-than-ideal way, we're wise to ask ourselves, "Did they pick this up from me? Are they mirroring what they see me do?"

Here are some examples to consider.

In Business

From a work perspective, I've seen this occur on several levels.

Supervisor: I witnessed a shift supervisor whose staff became lazy, took long breaks, and lost all loyalty toward the company. With the worst offenders fired, she hired and trained replacements. Yet, they fell into the same mode.

Investigating the supervisor revealed she had become lazy, took long breaks, and had no respect for her employer. Her charges merely followed her negative example.

Manager: I've also seen this happen to an entire office. It seemed that a good employee couldn't be found in the entire city. Each new hire turned out to be a liar, a manipulator, and a denigrator of company policy and procedure.

Alas, the manager was a compulsive liar, manipulated her staff, and showed contempt for company expectations.

A new manager found good employees to hire. The office slowly returned to functioning as it should.

Owner: I knew a company owner who complained about his terrible employees. The staff falsified timecards, stole supplies, lodged complaints, and even filed lawsuits. This perplexed the owner, but the cause was clear—even to a casual outsider. He under-reported income, cheated employees out of their pay, and threatened to sue everyone who irritated him.

Customers

Every business has a few challenging customers—the kind everyone wishes would go away. But if a company's clientele are all difficult, this warrants some tough introspection.

I once saw this dramatically demonstrated through an acquisition, where the prior owners were less than honorable with their customers. As the new owner, dealing with their client base was quite a challenge. It took several years to get the clients to stop yelling at managers, cursing staff, and challenging every bill.

But who was to blame them? They were simply matching how the former owner treated them.

Children

When parents see things in their children they don't like, they may do some soul searching and ask, "Where did they learn this?" Often, it's from the parents themselves.

Although children have many spheres of influence, parents are a key source—or at least they should be. The saying, "The apple doesn't fall far from the tree," is usually true.

Words can influence and direct, but actions are the prime training tool. What we do should reinforce what we say, sending a strong and consistent message, both at work and at home.

No one is perfect, but when a consistent trend of unacceptable behavior emerges from those closest to us, it might be time to look at our own actions as the possible underlying cause. After all, the things we do are nothing to sneeze about.

Life Lesson

Let's be a positive example to those around us.

APOLOGIZE

SAYING "I'M SORRY" IS GOOD FOR OTHERS
. . . AND FOR OURSELVES

Navigating the healthcare industry presents formidable challenges. And that's just to find the right provider who will, in theory, accept your insurance. Even worse is paying for the services once rendered. It always takes several months and often requires multiple contacts to plead, dispute, or clarify.

One time I had two outstanding medical invoices, which I'd been working on for several months. It would be far simpler to ignore the negotiated fees and pay the billed amount in full. But because I had healthcare insurance, I wanted to use it instead of capitulating to an unyielding bureaucracy that refused to correct their error. Right?

Another call to my provider quickly escalated

into a confrontation between me and the provider's rep. She threatened to turn me over to collections, while I begged them to allow me to pay the negotiated fee as payment in full. She would have none of it. I may have raised my voice. I may have said some things I'm not proud of. And I may have ended the call with a complete lack of restraint.

I hung up with equal parts frustration and remorse. Having failed at my mission to resolve the pending bill or even move the situation closer to resolution, I was even more distraught at my uncivil behavior.

Three days later, I had new information and called back for yet another attempt. Because they're a large organization, I'd never talked to the same person twice. I knew I'd reach a different rep this time.

Guess who answered the phone?

Yes, it was the same person I failed to treat with respect on my prior call. I groaned to myself when she shared her name. I had a split second to decide what to do. Should I humble myself and apologize for my errant words or ignore my prior behavior with arrogant justification?

I sucked in a lungful of courage and opened my mouth. "Hi!" I said as positively as possible. "I talked with you a few days ago and wasn't very nice. I'm sorry."

She didn't know what to say. Truly, she was speechless.

After a silence long enough to make me wonder if she was still there, she meekly said, "Um . . . thank you."

A weight lifted from my being. My tense shoulders released, and my muscles relaxed. The tightness in my chest eased. My soul lightened.

Though I couldn't undo my prior poor behavior, I had worked to amend it. Once accomplished, I felt better about myself and more distant from my past rudeness.

I don't know how the rep felt about the situation, but I hope my attempt to right my wrong made the rest of her day go a bit better. I hope my words of apology will help ease the sting of when the next person isn't nice to her.

Though I don't know if me saying I was sorry was a factor or not, that day we moved closer to a resolution. A month later my healthcare provider accepted my healthcare insurer's negotiated amount as payment in full.

We all know people who refuse to say, "I'm sorry." Maybe they're too proud. Perhaps they never learned how. Or might they not see a need to do so?

Other people do it wrong. I once knew a guy whose apologies were passive-aggressive. He'd say, "I'm sorry you misunderstood me," or "I'm sorry you didn't listen." He's getting better at giving a genuine apology, but at times he still struggles.

These various mindsets all reveal character flaws, but that's no excuse. When we make a mistake, the right thing to do is apologize.

Each time we say, "I'm sorry," makes it easier to do the next time we falter. That's how we grow as a person.

Life Lesson

We need to strive to live a life that requires no apology. But when we fall short, we must be quick to admit it and seek to restore the relationship.

BE NICE

EMBRACE THIS COMMONSENSE BUT OFT-FORGOTTEN INSTRUCTION

When children begin school, their teachers start by instilling in them the basics of how to behave in class and get along with others. These include learning how to be quiet and listen, to do what the teacher says, and to share with others. Other lessons cover no yelling, no hitting, and no biting. They need to learn to be nice to each other.

Students receive this foundational instruction in kindergarten—or at least they should. Yet it seems some never learned this critical life skill of being nice. And others appear to have forgotten it.

What a Nice Man

In the chapter "Apologize," I shared a time when I wasn't nice and needed to make amends for my errant words. Fortunately, rude behavior isn't my norm.

Another time I called a company, and we had what I deemed as a satisfactory, yet unremarkable, conversation. As we said our goodbyes, but before I could hang up, the agent sighed and whispered, "What a nice man."

My mind went spinning. First was the shock that she had voiced her opinion before disconnecting our call. Second was the realization that I'd done nothing special to earn the positive label she gave me. If my behavior stood out to her as being nice, I suspect many of her other callers must be the opposite. I shudder at what her workdays must be like.

Though I deserved little credit for it, I hoped the rest of her day was a bit better because of our interaction.

This thought encouraged me to be more intentional about being nice.

As restaurants reopened after the pandemic, I began thanking the staff, grateful that they had come back to work and were again preparing and serving food.

At sit-down restaurants, I affirm the waitstaff with my words and a nice tip. Then I thank the cashier or hostess as I leave.

At quick-serve restaurants (my more common destination), I approach the counter and share my appreciation as I leave. I say, "Thank you," smile, and wave. Sometimes I add "The food was great!" or "Have a nice day."

This surprises them. Every time.

My appreciation reverberates through the staff. Many reciprocate with wide smiles, waves, and delight. Their joyous reactions tells me they seldom receive appreciation from their patrons.

Likely assuming I couldn't hear him, once an employee whispered to a coworker, "What a nice man."

This was the second time someone called me a *nice man*. I like that label. May I always strive to be a nice man.

This experience also reinforced the importance of thanking people for their work. Simple actions can mean much. May we never forget this.

Training to Be Nice

A friend works for a company that helps government agencies improve their service. His team needs to address the basics. Sometimes they start with a simple instruction that should be common-sense in the service sector: "Be nice to the people you serve."

But some employees don't get it. Someone usually asks, "Why?"

The second step is to explain why it's important to be nice.

I'm incredulous that any customer service employee needs to be told to be nice, but apparently not everyone realizes it. These workers need to first learn this lesson, then master the concept, and finally apply it to the people they serve.

In customer service—as with life—*be nice* stands as a key foundational principle. The ability to be nice should stand as a requirement for hire. Companies should screen for this "skill" in the interview process. But if one person slips through who isn't nice, then they need to receive *Be Nice* training. What would this instruction entail?

Although it seems obvious, here are the key elements of what it takes to *Be Nice.*

Embrace the Golden Rule: The golden rule reminds us to "Do unto others as you would have them do unto you." This stands as the underlying principle for *Be Nice*. When we treat others as we wish to be treated, we take a huge first step toward being nice.

Smile: It's easier to be nice when we smile. And it's harder to be nice when we frown. So, remember to smile. And this doesn't just apply to in-person interactions. Smile when you're on a video call. Smile when you talk on the phone, for people can hear your smile.

Be Friendly: We've all encountered surliness in customer service situations, be it in-person, over the phone, or online. Don't be surly.

Surly repels, whereas friendly attracts. It's also much easier to be friendly when we smile, while unfriendly is more likely to follow a frown.

Respond Fast: Part of being nice is being responsive. In customer service situations, it's frustrating to have to wait for a preoccupied employee to give us their attention, but it happens all the time. We wait while they complete a trivial conversation with a coworker or wrap up a personal phone call.

Solve Problems: The main reason for customer service is to resolve customer issues, so the goal of *Be Nice* training is to solve problems. This includes resolving the issue and customers agreeing that we did.

We must embrace the golden rule in all aspects of our lives, not just for customer service. Extend these *Be Nice* goals to all our interactions. Smile, be friendly, respond fast, and be responsive.

Besides our customers, this applies to our employers, to our friends, and to our family—especially our family.

Be nice at work and be nice at home. Be nice to others, and they'll often be nice in return. But if they don't reciprocate, shake it off. That's on them.

Just be nice, and you'll have a positive impact everywhere you go, in everything you do, and to everyone around you.

Life Lesson

Let's be nice in all that we do.

BE FRIENDLY

REACH OUT TO OTHERS WHENEVER AND HOWEVER YOU CAN

B uilding on our prescription to be nice, we extend the concept to being friendly. It takes little effort to be friendly, yet it seems too many people do the opposite. They're self-absorbed, focusing on themselves and not on others. They look inward instead of outward.

Being friendly doesn't just apply to outgoing people, even though it might be easier for them. Everyone can—and should—be friendly. This applies to the introvert just as much as the extrovert. Each of us can be friendly in our own way.

As an introvert—along with a slight majority of the population—I may not be as outgoing as others, but I can still be friendly. For me, it starts with the simple act of waving to my neighbors, a lesson I learned through my father's example.

We live in a small 27-house subdivision. Our home is one of two that flank the entrance. Whenever I'm outside, I wave to my neighbors as they go by. I also try to include a smile as I do. Usually, they're driving. Sometimes they're on foot.

If I'm near the sidewalk as they walk by, we exchange a quick greeting. Sometimes they pause to talk. This adds to our interaction and deepens our connection.

Yet it's not just neighbors who receive my efforts at friendliness. I wave to everyone as they enter or leave our subdivision. Either they're my neighbor or they know my neighbor. Both deserve a friendly welcome. And most all wave back, even those who are visiting.

Many neighbors now intentionally turn their head toward our house as they drive by, checking to see if I'm out. This gives them the opportunity to wave first. It's affirming when they take the initiative.

Though some may think me odd for this prac- tice, I'd rather stand out as being affable than stand out as being aloof.

It takes more effort—especially for an introvert

—to be friendly in other settings, yet I strive to be friendly to people when I'm shopping or in public. The social environment I'm most often in is church. Some congregations are friendly, and some are not.

When my wife and I visited churches for my book *52 Churches*, the friendliness of some members stood out. Yet at too many congregations, everyone ignored us. No one said "Hi," and no one acknowledged our presence. It's as if we were invisible.

At most of these congregations, the people talked with their friends and those they knew, but they dismissed us and other visitors. Yes, at some churches, people made awkward efforts to connect with us, but at least they tried. I'd rather encounter an uneasy attempt than a stoic distance.

My takeaway from this experience is to look for visitors first.

When I serve as a greeter at church, my plan is a simple three-step process. I make eye contact, smile, and offer a handshake. Sometimes this last part becomes a fist bump or a high five. Regardless, we make a connection, albeit a brief one. Even an introvert like me can do this.

Yes, there are other ways to be friendly, with some people more talented at it than others. It's easier for some to be open, outgoing, and gracious.

Yet we can all be kind and pleasant with others. This is the essence of being friendly.

Life Lesson

We should all try to be friendly to whatever degree we can whenever we can. In doing so, we become more aware of others and help make their day go a bit better.

TAKE YOUR TURN

YIELDING TO OTHERS GIVES THEM A GIFT
AND COSTS US LITTLE

T he largest event venue in our area is downtown. It requires finding a place to park and paying for the privilege. My family and I always use a parking ramp that offers convenient access to the venue and isn't as exorbitant as other options.

To access the ramp, however, requires us making a left-hand turn into the only entrance. With oncoming traffic always present, this could present a daunting challenge. Yet it does not.

The first time I encountered this dilemma, I waited behind a string of cars waiting to turn left to park. I quickly surmised I'd not be able to use this ramp and would need to seek another place to park. Yet what I saw amazed me. It still does.

Though many of the oncoming cars drove by the ramp, the car next in line to make a right-hand turn into the ramp motioned to the next car in the left-hand turn lane to go first. Then they followed. The car behind them offered the same courtesy.

Driver after driver repeated this pattern, car after car.

In no time at all our car sat in front of the left-turn lane. The driver next up in the right-turn lane, with his turn signal on, motioned for me to go first. I did, and then he followed.

Over the years, we've gone to many events at this arena and have always parked in this ramp, experiencing this same courtesy every time. Only once did I ever witness this unexpected civility not happen. The driver waiting to make a right-hand turn inched his vehicle forward, as if glued to the car ahead of him. He had every right to go next, and he took it. The driver after him, however, reverted to this uncommon practice.

There are, of course, many scenarios when we can take turns or let someone go first. Though these can occur while we're in our car, many more opportunities present themselves when we're on foot. It takes little time or effort to gesture for someone to go before us.

Though I sometimes forget to do this, I succeed more often than I fail. Doing so offers others a gift.

Since it's more blessed to give than to receive, I enjoy a blessing each time I do.

When we insist on going next, we place ourselves—our needs, agenda, and schedule—above others. When we let others go before us, we honor them with undeserved kindness.

What a delightful way to go through life. It costs us little and offers them much. And each time we give this simple gift to others, we feel a bit better about ourselves.

Life Lesson

Let's seek opportunities to take turns or let others go first.

BE QUICK TO FORGIVE

OFFERING FORGIVENESS IS A GIFT TO THE
OFFENDER . . . AND TO YOURSELF

B esides writing books and blog posts, I produce trade publications for the call center industry. At one time, I printed copies of my magazines. I'd mail these to subscribers and occasionally pass them out at industry conventions and trade shows.

Several years ago, the marketing manager at one of our largest advertisers placed a picture of his company's president on the front cover of our flag-ship magazine, with the understanding it would be distributed at the industry's leading annual convention.

I attended that event.

Yet the team that ran the convention didn't

distribute my magazines to attendees. I needed to find out why and fix it. Here's what I learned:

The magazines weren't distributed because the association hadn't received them. The association hadn't received them because the printer hadn't shipped them to the conference center. And the printer hadn't shipped them because I forgot to order extra copies. Even if I asked them to rush a second print run, the copies wouldn't arrive until after the convention ended.

It was all my fault, and there was nothing I could do to fix it. It stands as my biggest blunder as a periodical publisher.

I went to the president of the company in question to report what I learned, to explain why the magazine promoting his image and his company's message wasn't passed out to the attendees as promised.

Though I don't remember what I said, I think it was along the lines of, "The magazines weren't passed out because I forgot to order extra copies. I'm sorry."

I expected him to be upset, to be mad at me. He had every right to be. It was all my fault. But that wasn't the reaction I received, not at all.

Calm washed over his demeanor. His eyes

emoted kindness. In the gentlest of responses, he breathed four words I'll never forget. "Peter, I forgive you." These words flowed with compassion, covered with love.

Relief flooded my being. He granted me mercy, even though I deserved none. Telling me he forgave me was the biggest gift he could offer.

Though this happened many years ago, the memory of his response still makes me misty eyed.

I can't confirm the source—though it may have been Marianne Williamson—who shared astute wisdom about offering forgiveness: "Unforgiveness is like drinking poison yourself and waiting for the other person to die."

An alternate version states, "Holding a grudge is like drinking poison and hoping the other person dies." Nursing a grudge is the outcome of holding on to unforgiveness.

When we forgive others for their mistakes—for their errors that affect us—we negate a poison that would hurt us if we kept it contained.

We must, therefore, forgive others who wrong us. We should do so quickly and fully. It's for their benefit . . . and for ours.

Life Lesson

When we forgive others who have hurt us, we offer them a gift and benefit ourselves. They receive mercy, and we free ourselves from holding onto a destructive emotion.

LESSONS FROM THE GAME OF CHESS

IT'S YOUR MOVE

My cousins taught me how to play chess when I was in third grade. Having just learned checkers the year before, my parents, doubting I could grasp the complexities of the game, urged caution and tried to lower my expectations. Yet I forged ahead.

My oldest cousin patiently taught me the names of the pieces and how they moved. He gently quizzed me to gauge my understanding. Soon we played an actual game. Despite novice errors, I had a great time. We played until he grew weary. Then I begged his brother for a few games. But he had less tolerance for my sloppy play. By midafternoon, we moved on to other things.

The next morning, I challenged my instructor

to play again. Before the day was done, I won my first game. He rallied, winning the next two, but I sensed I was challenging him. By the time their visit was over, I was hooked on the game.

Practice Makes Perfect

Despite my strong desire to play chess, I had few opportunities. I asked family members, but each had a reason not to learn the game. My neighbor wasn't much help either, having only a passing interest.

So I played against myself.

Sometimes I would play white (which moves first and takes the offense). Other times I would take the black side (which responds and defends). Sometimes, I'd switch sides midway through the game, giving up a superior position to assume a lesser one.

These exercises may not have been the best way to improve, but I did get better. When it came time for a proper game, my practicing paid off.

Study

Although enjoyable, playing against myself became wearisome. So I turned to books. First, I learned some esoteric rules, like *en passant*, which is seldom used in an actual game. Then I studied opening moves and their recommended defenses. I also learned techniques, like the pin, the knight fork (a personal favorite), discovered check (a great way to confound your opponent), and gambits, as well as endgame tactics.

Having consumed several books, I zeroed in on one titled *How to Beat Bobby Fischer*. The premise was that it was statistically more probable to beat Fischer than to force a draw—of course, he was nine times more likely to win than lose. I read, studied, and reenacted many of the sixty-one games he lost in Grandmaster tournaments. I reasoned that to improve, I needed to study the master.

Don't Give Up

In high school, the unspoken credo among my chess-playing buddies was that you never conceded. No matter how dire the situation, we would never quit, playing to the end. Resigning a chess game was for those of lesser character. This perspective taught me two things.

First, I learned how to be a good winner, to be gracious to the other player as a person, all the while dismantling his army and backing his king into the corner for an acrimonious checkmate. I wanted to win but desired to not belittle my opponent in the process. After all, I would want to play him again.

Playing to the end also taught me to remain dignified in defeat. That's much harder—especially when the vanquishing conqueror is relishing his impending victory too much. Yet, these moments perfect character.

Play It Again

Losing is never fun, especially when you deem yourself the superior player, but it happens. I learned to accept defeat as part of the game and to grow in the process. It's true that you can learn more in defeat than in victory.

It's also important to not wallow in self-pity when setbacks occur but to shake off the disappointment and forge into the future. Regardless of how close I came to winning or how big the loss, my first response was invariably, "Wanna play again?"

React Quickly

Sometimes we'd play "rapid chess," where you had to move within five seconds. With no timer, it was self-policing. It taught us to think astutely and react quickly. I had a knack for it, able to assess a situation and make a snap decision, sometimes based on intuition. Games only lasted about five minutes and were so intense that it only took a couple to give me a headache.

I sometimes adopted a rapid-chess strategy in a regular game. Although my hurried moves were not always ideal, their unending swiftness unnerved my opponent, causing him to get flustered and make blunders. From his perspective, it was always his turn, and he was always intently concentrating. I, however, could relax and have fun.

I learned it was often better to make a quick decision that was good than to take time to make a move that was better.

To imply that life is like a game of chess is a shallow metaphor. Yet just as a good game of chess requires an intentional approach and sound strategy, so does living a worthwhile life.

Life Lesson

Let's apply these lessons from chess to our lives. It's your move. What's it going to be?

MONEY MANAGEMENT
CONTROL YOUR FINANCES OR THEY WILL CONTROL YOU

From an early age, a lesson I learned well from my parents was to spend money with care and exercise financial responsibility. As a result, I've never lived beyond my means, as so many people do today.

Though I lived for a time at my level of income, I quickly decided to live below my means. Remember, money is not a goal to aim for or a scorecard to brag about. Instead, it's a means to provide for our needs.

Here's my financial plan:

Spend

I determined to live a lifestyle simpler than I could afford. I decided to only spend some of my money. This allowed me to have funds to save and to share.

Save

At first, I saved to have a financial safety net. Once established, I then saved for major purchases, paying by cash and avoiding credit. Later I added saving for retirement to the mix.

These all allowed me to live a financially responsible life. I've planned, and I've prepared. What a burden this lifts from me when I look toward the future.

Share

The third area of finances is charity. It's giving some money away. This doesn't mean donating a portion of excess funds. Instead, it's to plan for and be prepared to give to needs. We'll talk about this further in the chapter on generosity.

My parents modeled using money for these three areas as I grew up. But they didn't state it. They just did it.

Joyce Meyer, however, succinctly summarizes this plan—which she and her husband follow—as "spend some, save some, and give some."

Notice she doesn't state amounts or percentages but leaves it open-ended. This means it's for us to decide. The only ratio I find unacceptable is 100-0-0. That's both shortsighted and selfish. Don't be that person.

For myself, I began working toward a goal of 80-10-10. It took a while to get there. I then worked to move beyond that and will continue to do so.

Life Lesson

We need to treat money as a tool to live responsibly and help others.

ARE YOU TOO BUSY?

GIVE PRIORITY TO WHAT MATTERS MOST

Perhaps you've heard this story.

Picture a large college classroom, one with tiered seating, able to accommodate hundreds of students. The students assemble in expectation.

At exactly 8 o'clock, the professor strides in. Without acknowledging the learners, he reaches under the lectern and produces a gallon glass jar. He sets it on a nearby table. Then he pulls out a box of rocks and places it next to the jar. Finally, he fixes his gaze on his students. Garnering their attention, he clears his throat, gestures to the rocks, and asks, "Who would like to show us how much you can fit in?"

An eager-to-impress freshman shoots up his

hand. Desiring to make an impression, Mr. Eager-to-Impress carefully places rocks in the jar.

"Is the jar full?" The professor asks.

"Yes!" the students reply in unison.

"Can you fit any more in?"

"No!"

Then the instructor produces a bag of pebbles. The students gasp. A hush falls over the room. Mr. Eager-to-Impress is in a quandary. Should he keep quiet and retreat or attempt to salvage his bravado? Hesitantly, he raises his hand and then comes forward. With great care, he places a handful of pebbles at the top. By tapping, shaking, and rotating the jar, they make their way to many of the gaps below. Satisfied with the results, he returns to his chair, hoping for the best.

"Is the jar full now?"

"Um, yes," the students answer.

"Can you fit any more in?"

"No," they answer, but with hesitation.

Next, the instructor brings out a pail of sand. Many students smile. "How about now?" Eager-to-Impress is not so eager anymore, but feels his fate is already decided. Without being asked, he slinks back to the table. Using the same technique, he filters the sand through the courser maze of rocks and pebbles. Red-faced, he sits down, eager for class to end.

With a smile, the teacher asks, "Is the jar full now?"

No one ventures a response. Whatever they might say could be wrong. Besides, no one wants to stand out like Eager-to-Impress.

The professor ignores their silence. "Can you fit any more in the jar?"

More silence.

The learners squirm in the moment's hush. Without saying a word, the teacher reaches under the podium and brings forth a pitcher of water. Some students groan. Others laugh.

The educator grins. Slowly, he pours the water into the jar, permeating every crevice. He fills it to the top and then overflows it. There's no doubt whether the jar is full.

"What can we learn from this?"

Eager-to-Impress, wanting to salvage something from this debacle, summons his courage. "It means that no matter how busy we are, we can always fit more in!"

"No!" the professor bellows. "It means that unless you do the big things first, they'll never get done!"

I've heard several variations of this story. Since I don't know who wrote it, I share my version with a nod to "Anonymous."

Personally, I'm adept at handling the pebbles and sand in my life, topping it off with an abundant supply of water to make things seem full. I must, however, be intentional to handle the rocks, those important tasks. Without deliberate action, I put off the big stuff until tomorrow, attending to life's minutia today. In doing so, I often fail to tackle its priorities.

We're busy at work and leave to be busy at home. We're busy in recreation and busier still on vacation. We return to work needing to rest. Our busyness distracts us from what's important, from what really matters, from those things that could truly make a difference.

Life Lesson

We will do well to address the big things in our lives and let go of the trivial.

RECLAIM YOUR LIFE

SEVEN STEPS TO REDUCE STRESS AND INCREASE JOY

I've pondered my busyness and am working toward a cure. Here are seven steps I pursue to reduce my stress and increase my joy.

1. Rethink Time Management

The thrust of time management is controlling how we spend our hours to allow us the space to do more. This doesn't bring relief. It just means squeezing more into an already full day. Turn time management on its head. Use it to control how we spend our time—to do *less*, not more.

Just do the tasks that matter most.

2. Avoid Multitasking

When we multitask, we're not really doing two things at once but merely quickly switching back and forth. Personally, I fear my past pursuit of multitasking only threatened to give me ADD. Not only is multitasking counter-productive, but there's also evidence it messes up our brains. Don't do it.

3. Keep a Time Log

I used to periodically ask my managers to keep a time log for a week. I'd do it too. They hated it, and so did I, but the results were instructive, documenting our wasted time and misplaced priorities.

Work aside, let's look at some easy time wasters. How much TV do you watch a day? How much time do you spend on social media? This amounts to hours that could be put to a different use, attending to the big things, not squandered in passive activities of no real consequence.

While we all need to relax, if we weren't so perpetually busy, we wouldn't need so much time to escape.

4. Just Say No

We tell our kids to say "no" to unwise behaviors and we would do well to heed our own advice. Sometimes it's wise to say "no" to good things to protect us from over-committing and ending up too busy to do anything well.

5. Set Limits

My tolerance for work used to be about 50 to 55 hours a week. If things ballooned beyond that, out of self-preservation, I'd cut back until I again had a tolerable schedule. If I self-police to a 55-hour workweek, I theorized I could learn to limit myself to 45. It took some time, but I did it.

In looking at my output and quality during those 45-hour workweeks, I saw nothing that suffered. I was also more relaxed, less stressed, and had more free time.

6. Know Yourself

My default mode is to handle the pebbles and sand at the beginning of my day and attend to the rocks in the afternoon—if there's time. (See "Are You

Too Busy?") This isn't wise, as my greatest focus and peak energy occur in the morning.

This means that without intentional fore-thought, I handle trivial tasks when I'm at my best, while reserving important work for my low point. I've noted a similar cycle throughout the week and another that's seasonal.

It takes concerted effort, but I now strive to prioritize key tasks for peak times, while delegating lesser activities to my lower energy moments.

7. Do the Big Things

Once we take steps to control life's activities, we can attend to the big things. Without the pressures of trivial concerns, there's freedom to focus on the important, the life altering, and the significant. Doing so removes us from the rut that all too easily goes from day to day, week to week, month to month, and year to year—all without noticeable progress.

Life Lesson

We need to control our time and our schedule, or else it will control us.

SOCIAL MEDIA
DISTRACTING, DIVISIVE, AND DANGEROUS

When I set up my first social media account, I followed a few close friends and endeavored to read every one of their posts. That didn't last long. As the number of my connections grew, the quantity of posts soon had me feeling overwhelmed.

Then I added a second platform and, after that, several more. It's an unmanageable amount of information. I make no effort to keep up to date.

Long ago, I turned off all notifications. If I have time, I proactively check a couple of my social media pages once each weekday—and only once a day—as I wrap up my work. I peek in on a few more once a week and some just once a month. I shut down a few and said good riddance. What a relief.

There are times I wonder about closing them all. I think I would, except that I use a few for advertising and might one day want to tap into others.

Aside from running occasional promotions, I use social media to point to my website, my writing hub. I treat my website as my online home, with my social media pages as mere spokes on the wheel, funneling a bit of traffic to my online home.

Beyond that, I see little value in social media. It's a distraction at best and a seductive danger at worst.

Experts from various fields decry the downsides of social media, especially on young minds. But that doesn't make adults impervious to its risks.

It seems little content has true significance. Many of the postings are people trumpeting the very best parts of their lives, elevating themselves in the process and leaving out the negative—except for those going through a crisis who seek support or sympathy.

Then there are the snarky and hateful comments by people who have nothing better to do. They stir up dissension, start arguments, and sow division. Frankly, I don't need the negativity in my life. No one does.

Next are the bots, posing as real people but pursuing some nefarious agenda. Let's not forget all the spam messages directed specifically at us.

Last, there are many people who use social media as their news source, but it's most unreliable in that regard. Posts are apt to provide wrong information or biased perspectives.

That's why I limit my social media interactions and have deprioritized it as a useful tool in connecting with my audience. I use my website and newsletter for that, not social media. Let's not lose sight of this.

Also, you should never set up your home base on a social media platform. It can be summarily removed, leaving you with no recourse to reclaim it or communicate with your followers.

Let's seek personal one-on-one interaction in real life with real people. Aside from that, we can tap email, text, and the telephone as optional communication tools. But to the degree possible, let's leave social media out of the mix.

We must limit our use of social media and its role in our lives. We'll be better off when we do.

Life Lesson

If we don't limit our use of social media, it will limit us.

THE TRUTH ABOUT COLLEGE
ADVANCED EDUCATION MAY NOT MATTER
AS MUCH AS YOU THINK

I t amuses me to tell people I went to college for thirty-eight years. Their reactions vary from shock to admiration.

As a high school sophomore, I learned the local community college would admit select high school seniors. Acting partly out of youthful arrogance and partly from moxie, I met with an admissions counselor, hoping to be admitted the following year. The advisor never asked my age or my grade as he mechanically pulled my high school transcript. Mathematically challenged, he failed to convert my school's quarterly grades into the semester credits he usually saw. "Well," he concluded, "it sure looks like you have enough credits."

I completed my first college class before I started my junior year of high school. I took at least one class a semester for the next two years. College offered a challenge that high school lacked. Though I earned high marks in high school, I excelled in my college courses.

As my senior year of high school wound down, classmates announced their college plans. My best friend chose a private school to study a new field called computer science. It seemed an interesting and promising choice, and I wanted to go there too.

Yet, despite my parents having sacrificed to make weekly deposits into my college fund since the day I was born, the balance fell far short. This reality, coupled with frequent media reports of college graduates being under-employed in entry-level positions, led me to make a more practical decision.

I enrolled in an electronics technical school where—for a fraction of the cost—I could quickly learn practical job skills and enter the workforce in a couple of years. Upon graduation, I grabbed the first job that came along: repairing copy machines.

Quickly Dismissed

It soon became apparent this was not the job for me. My electronics school credential read, "Electronic Engineering Technician." Though I fancied myself an engineer, prospective employers viewed me as a technician. To make the career change I wanted, I needed more education. I reapplied to the community college and earned a pre-engineering degree.

Upon graduating, I transferred to a local university and enrolled in its electrical engineering program. Yet well before graduation, a job change took me out of state. I established residency there and resumed my education. During this time, I responded to a help wanted ad. The stated salary was three times what I currently made.

I met every qualification and dashed off my resume, fully expecting to be hired. But they didn't even interview me. I later learned the company was deluged with applications and summarily rejected every applicant without a four-year college degree, even though the job didn't require one.

I resolved to never let that happen again.

Any Degree Is Better than None

Now being cynically convinced that a college degree was little more than an attendance certificate, I sought the shortest path to a four-year degree. I found the perfect solution, one geared toward full-time workers who had at least two years of college. By attending evening classes in an intense one-year program, I could parlay my various college credits with documented experiential learning into a bachelor's degree.

I didn't care what the degree was in. I just wanted that piece of paper. As the school year wound down, however, I was met with a surprise at work. In my annual review, my boss told me my management skills had greatly improved. He rewarded me with a substantial raise. Although I had been striving for an arbitrary credential, I inadvertently ended up improving my job skills.

I shared this news with my professor, thanking him profusely. In what seemed unwarranted humility, he dismissed my gratitude. "I don't deserve any credit," he said. "All we did was offer you an opportunity. It was up to you to make something of it. What you have inside you made the difference." It was years before I fully comprehended this.

Now, seeing a direct connection between education and earning power, I returned for a second major. What I had previously learned were *soft* skills (interpersonal communication, group dynamics, human resources, and so forth). Now I needed to complement this with course work in accounting, business law, and strategic planning. This major, business administration, would enhance my job skills, making me a better and more marketable employee.

A Master's and a Doctorate

After a few years, missing the elixir of education and feeling inadequate as a manager, I began considering a master's degree. Again, I found a program geared toward non-traditional students. Their offer was compelling, but even more intriguing was that I could enroll in a joint master's/doctorate program. I did. I expected the master's degree would make me complete as a manager, but I viewed the doctorate more as a personal milestone.

After completing my master's degree as planned, I immediately began working on the doctorate, which I had two years to complete.

Already worn down by the intensity of the master's, I soon regretted committing to the doctoral program. But stubbornness prevailed, and I plodded on, meeting the requirements only a few months before the deadline. I was forty-two. It was twenty-six years since I had gotten a jumpstart in college at age sixteen.

There were some diversions along the way: marriage, children, job changes, relocations, and even a few breaks, but for much of that time, I attended classes—somewhere.

A Second Doctorate

Fast forward a few more years. I felt a prompting to return to school once again. This time for personal edification, picking a Bible college—again through distance learning. I applied for a second doctorate, but they didn't accept me. Not caring about the credential, but the learning opportunity, I accepted placement in their master's program.

Yet a couple of classes into it, during a routine call to the school, I learned they had undergone a change in how they evaluated transfer credits. They bumped me up to their "second doctorate" program, which for me required fewer classes than the master's program I was in. And it cost less too. I switched. By graduation, I had spent nearly thirty-eight years in college. And that's more than enough college for me.

What College Means

College has meant many things to me: a challenge, a means to a job, help with a career change, an attendance certificate, an avenue to a better salary, an enhancer of job skills, management training, and personal edification. College can be many things depending on what we need and what we want to accomplish, but it is not a cure-all.

When I worked as a call center consultant, I would do week-long business audits. I'd begin on Monday with an overview of the client's company and then move to uncover weaknesses and opportunities.

In doing so, a distressing pattern emerged. On about the third day, I'd often find myself in a follow-up meeting with the call center manager. They'd share their common concern in different ways and with various levels of emotion, but it always boiled down to the same sentiment: "I feel inadequate as a manager. I think I need a college degree."

This broke my heart. I was never sure what to say.

These were successful, dynamic women, who started at entry-level positions and—through hard work, dedication, and a talent for doing what's nearly impossible—rose to significant positions. These individuals oversaw most of their organization's workforce, controlled about half of its expenses (primarily labor costs), and maintained virtually all the company revenue, yet they still felt inadequate.

They believed a degree would make everything right. This always caught me by surprise because they conducted their work with such great aplomb, confidence, and success.

Here's what I should have told them: "Yes, college can help you. If you can go and are willing to make the sacrifices of time and money, while putting much of your life on hold, then do it. It will make you a better manager. But it isn't a panacea. There will still be times when you'll feel overwhelmed, inadequate, or unprepared. Most managers have these feelings, and a formal education won't make them go away."

While my educational choices have, in part, enabled me to get to where I am today, I know that had I taken a different path, the result would be no less meaningful, because, as my college professor said, "It's what you have inside that makes the difference."

What If You Don't Already Have a Career?

These comments about college apply to those who have a full-time job. For the recent high school graduate and those just starting out or without a career path, college *may* be the right option, provided you can handle the cost and the workload.

Being a traditional student and going to school full-time allows you to get a degree in the shortest time, but it is not financially possible for everyone. In this case, intersperse education with vocation. Although this approach takes longer, it enhances the experience, as education complements work, while work magnifies education.

With college costs, however, increasing at about twice the rate of inflation, year after year, it's becoming increasingly inaccessible for many. Add to this the reality that many people don't end up working in the field their college classes prepare them for. Or they do so only for a short time before switching careers into one that doesn't require a degree.

My advice is that if you want a career that requires a degree—such as being a nurse, doctor, accountant, engineer, or teacher—go to college. Otherwise, give serious consideration to non-college educational or job preparatory options.

What If You Have No Idea What to Study?

If you lack a career vision, be sure to pursue marketable job skills. But don't focus on maximizing your earning potential. Instead, look at what is marketable *and* will maximize your enjoyment of life, which is not money.

For those who are analytical thinkers, business and technology fields are good pursuits. For creative minds, consider marketing or graphic arts.

Be aware that most college graduates don't end up working in the field they studied. Instead, they use their education as an entry-point into the workforce. Once you have successfully proven yourself in full-time employment, work history becomes more important than your degree.

Life Lesson

If you go to college, study hard and make the most of the opportunity. And if college isn't right for you, pursue a different path to meaningful employment.

Either way, it's what's inside us that makes the difference.

LEARN FROM HISTORY

TAP OTHERS FOR ADVICE, SUPPORT, AND ENCOURAGEMENT

O ne of the college assignments I most enjoyed was analyzing case studies. I relished learning from them, both the successes and the failures.

Not surprisingly, I take most seriously the adage, "Those who fail to learn from history are doomed to repeat it."

In business, the best histories to learn from are case studies, especially those accounts of the downfall, demise, or defeat of once-prosperous businesses or successful entrepreneurs. Of course, scrutinizing the steps taken in a remarkable turnaround are also instructive, as well as encouraging for anyone faced with a formidable uphill battle.

Although case studies of successes illuminate as well, offering encouragement to persevere, they're not nearly as instructive as learning from others through their shortfalls and their struggles.

Besides reading case studies, we can also hire consultants for personal direction. I did this when I went into magazine publishing. And I still hire consultants now for book promotion and marketing.

On the personal side, we can tap mentors, coaches, and counselors to help us navigate life's struggles. In doing so, we can avoid making the same mistakes as those who have gone before us.

Whether in business or in our personal lives, regardless of the situations we face, know that someone has encountered it before. Don't struggle with a problem as though it's unique; it is not. Do some research, read some books, and ask for help.

There's no need to go through difficulties alone. We'll do well to seek advice and support from others who have gone before us. We can struggle in isolation, or we can learn from others and do things the easy way.

Life Lesson

Whatever we do, we must learn from history so we don't repeat it.

UNDER THE INFLUENCE

MAKE A DIFFERENCE FOR THOSE
AROUND US

My daughter is a teacher. Over the years, she's taught every level from pre-school to eighth grade.

In her first year out of college, she taught first grade, influencing the next generation. I don't recall much about my first-grade teacher. But I do know I really liked her. Many times, my parents said Mrs. Frank gave me a great start in school, a sound foundation on which future teachers could build.

Another standout educator was Miss Robinson, for fourth grade. Our class was a challenge to her— a good one. Many of us had been in a split third/fourth-grade room the year before. Once our third-grade assignments were complete, we could do fourth-grade work.

As a result, Miss Robinson inherited a batch of students who had already mastered much of the fourth-grade curriculum. She worked hard to provide us with additional lessons to challenge us, without similarly handicapping our fifth-grade teacher.

My family moved that summer, and I started a new school. I quickly realized three things. I was far ahead in math, hopelessly behind in grammar, and placed in the wrong class by the school secretary.

Teachers often give more attention to students on the fringes, both those with great promise and those who struggle. My understanding of things unknown by my peers catapulted me to a position of prominence. As a result, my teacher gave me extra attention, while my classmates viewed me with academic awe.

Although I learned little that year, I underwent a metamorphosis of self-perception. Succinctly stated, I began fifth grade as an above-average student who felt average and ended the year as an above-average student convinced he was exceptional. That single change in attitude altered the trajectory of my life. Yes, Mrs. Wedel influenced me immensely.

In seventh grade, I had Mr. Snow for English.

He loved to teach, and he loved seventh graders. He invested extra effort in me during lunch and after school, striving to catch me up with grammar. Our class read and studied Dickens's classic story, *A Christmas Carol*.

Mr. Snow helped us dig into this timeless tale and mine its many truths. The conclusion was inescapable for me and equally profound. Like Dickens's Scrooge, we have a choice on how we live our life. We can be selfish, or we can embrace the joy of living, for ourselves and for the benefit of others. I chose the latter.

That year I also had Mr. Binder for science. He was a strict educator with high expectations—and I feared him—at least in class. Yet he also faithfully served as my track coach in junior high and high school, where he functioned in a much different role and with significant impact. On the track, I learned many of life's important lessons and that was where I experienced my happiest moments as a teen. Although I fell short in athletic ability, athletic opportunities helped to shape me more than anything learned in the classroom.

In high school, it was Mr. Grosser who affected me greatly. With a passion for molding young minds, he was part educator and part entertainer.

In his class, the unexpected became routine. Sometimes he addressed course material. At other times, he digressed. Regardless, he pushed us to think. His influence was significant, and it helped me mature as an individual and prepared me for adulthood.

The standout mentor of my college years was Professor Britten. Intellectual and insightful, he communicated profundity with ease. I hung on every word. Nothing he said was wasted; everything had significance. I took his classes, not because of the subject, but because of the instructor.

These teachers influenced me greatly. They stand out as the best of the best. Aside from academia, I have had many *teachers* in the business world and even more in my personal life. Although not typical educators, each guided me to become the person I am today.

If you're a teacher, be encouraged that you are influencing others—even if you don't know it. Those in your class may never affirm you, but you are making a difference to every student every year.

If you're not working in education, know that you, too, influence others. Whether in business, through social settings, or at home, you influence those around you by what you do, the things you say, and the way you treat others.

Like Scrooge, we can influence negatively by pursuing a life of selfish greed, or we can influence positively by choosing to make a difference in the lives of others. Although they may seldom thank us for our influence in their lives, we make a lasting impact.

We must strive to make the most out of each opportunity, and everyone will benefit. That includes them, you, me, and the world we live in.

Life Lesson

Let's seek to have positive influences in our lives and to be a positive influence on others.

WE CAN ALL USE A LITTLE HELP
SEEK ASSISTANCE WHEN NEEDED

"Y**ou** need a hobby!" My wife was exasperated. I don't recall the circumstances, but it's safe to assume I did something that irritated her. Regardless of the cause, her impromptu advice gave me pause.

Yes, a pastime, a relaxing diversion, would be good, but what should I do? I considered several options but dismissed each one for various reasons.

Word Challenges

I had a passing, yet ongoing, attraction to crossword puzzles. Though I rarely picked one up and never completed any, crossword puzzles seemed like a worthy pursuit. They'd nicely complement my interest in words and my goal to use them to encourage, inspire, and entertain.

Yes, I concluded, crossword puzzles would be my new hobby. I began looking for these word challenges, setting aside time for them. With consistent effort, I reasoned I would improve. I was wrong. Even with my initiative, my skills did not advance.

The turning point came by chance on an airplane, of all places. As I puzzled over the seemingly impossible offering in the inflight magazine, I sensed my seatmate reading over my shoulder. Finally, no longer able to contain herself, she gently whispered, "You should know 12 down."

I looked at the clue anew and an answer formed. I voiced my suspicion. With a pleased smile, she confirmed it to be correct. Immediately, she apologized for intruding, but I assured her I appreciated her help.

Though she attempted to distract herself, a few minutes later, my perplexing puzzle again captivated her attention. I slid the magazine in her direction, allowing us to both see it. She quickly directed my attention to another clue, encouraged me to think in a different direction, and then confirmed my uncertain answer.

A retired schoolteacher, one of her many interests was crossword puzzles. She shared with me tips to discern a puzzle's theme and how to tap into it. She gave advice on deciphering seemingly arcane clues and cutting through the deceit of intentionally misleading references.

Soon we had most of the puzzle complete. In an hour, she gave me the direction I needed to improve my skills and increase my enjoyment of my new hobby.

Horticulture

Another interest I have is plants, one instilled in me by my parents, but I only gave it passing attention for many years. My home's landscape once consisted only of green grass and a few strategically placed trees. Inside the house sat one miniature orange tree and a lone aloe plant. (Aloe pops up often in crossword puzzles.)

To increase the greenery inside and add color outside, I tapped into my slumbering fascination with plants. Again, I needed guidance, and my parents provided it. Over time, my yard morphed into an abundance of carefully selected plants and shrubs, designed to add color and beauty throughout the growing season. My indoor collection also expanded.

Work

We all need guidance in many areas, not just hobbies. When I embarked on a consulting career many years ago, several people gave me sage advice.

Three stand out. One was an industry friend who helped me clarify a transition strategy and first-year game plan. Another was an industry consultant who shared years of experiences and warned of common pitfalls. The third was a consultant in a parallel industry who gave expert recommendations for a pricing strategy. Together, these folks shortened my learning curve and paved the way to success.

In similar fashion, when I bought a magazine business, the sellers provided valuable guidance. I also tapped a publishing insider and contracted with an industry guru who quickly got me up to speed on standard practices.

The point is that I got help from many people—and continue to do so. With some, it's a formal arrangement. With others, it's more free flowing. In all cases, however, they help me advance faster and achieve better outcomes.

No person can know everything or excel in all areas. If someone else can help us, we should tap into his or her expertise. It's foolish to plod forward on our own.

Life Lesson

We can all use a little help and are wise to take it.

THE RIPPLE EFFECT

CONSIDER HOW YOUR LIFE AFFECTS
OTHERS

I 'd been thinking about it for quite some time. That little voice inside, however, said, "Today is the day." It seemed simple enough. I wanted to move the computer monitor on my desk a whopping eighteen inches.

When I first set up my office, I spent a lot of time finding the optimum configuration. Yet over time, things changed. New technology arrived, I updated equipment, and my business's scale increased. With each change, it never seemed the ideal time to consider the overall flow and function of my workspace.

My immediate goal was always the same: find a place for it now and make it work as quickly as possible. It's sad that even as an advocate of productivity, I allowed my workspace effectiveness to deteriorate. It seemed there were days when chaos was the rule rather than the exception.

One change that occurred during this slide into disarray was switching from a laptop computer to a desktop. The desktop monitor didn't fit my desk like the laptop had. If I placed the monitor in front of the monitor stand, it was too close. If I set the monitor on the stand, it was too high. In the moment's immediacy, I set the monitor to the left of the stand, intending to figure out a better solution when things slowed down.

This *temporary* position caused me to twist my body whenever I used my computer, which was most of the time. This wasn't ideal for posture or comfort.

I estimated that it would take about fifteen minutes (which I rounded up to an hour, just to be safe) to remove the monitor stand from my desk and slide the monitor to the right.

Today is the day, my inner voice proclaimed. After I processed the morning email, I slid under my desk to remove the monitor stand. Five minutes later, it sat on the floor in the middle of my office.

Ahead of schedule, I eased the monitor across the desk toward its new home. Yet after traveling only six inches, it came to an abrupt halt. The cable was too short. What should I do? Go to Plan B (which was yet to be determined) or return to my original configuration (which was unacceptable)?

Although buying a longer monitor cable was the solution, I wanted instant results.

Just move the computer, I concluded. To do this, however, I needed to first relocate the printer. That also made space for some shelving bins, which had been another "someday" project. I could use some bins that held past issues of my magazines. I'd simply move the extra copies to storage.

That effort prompted me to inventory past issues (no need to keep so many copies), throw extras away, and reorganize my archives. A half hour later, I was back in my office. One thing led to another and then another. Three hours into the project, with objects scattered everywhere, I scarcely had room to move.

I finally got the computer hooked up and work-ing, but *I* couldn't work. Things were in too much disarray. By the time I was done, six hours had passed. I'd moved every item on my desk (and shifted a few things twice), rearranged most of my file cabinet contents, made multiple trips to the garbage, re-prioritized my pending work, disconnected an unneeded gadget, cleaned up some wayward wiring, and even cancelled some phone services I wasn't using. Wow!

Though it took several hours, the results were worth it. I became more efficient and effective. I felt in control of my work, rather than controlled by it.

Did all this happen merely because I moved my monitor? Indirectly, yes. Relocating my monitor had a ripple effect, one I'd feel—and appreciate—for a long time.

No Ripples

Some people never experience this ripple effect. They plod from day to day, month to month, and year to year without ever giving a thought to the incapacitating office developing around them. Things get squeezed in here, hooked up there, and stacked on top, until routine work becomes an illogical series of unneeded steps or wasted activity. Their work becomes harder, but change seems harder still. Taking time to make things more efficient is inconceivable for them.

Too Many Ripples

The converse is people who make changes often, seemingly for fun or out of compulsion. They spend hours restructuring their office and do so about once a month. Yet this investment occurs so often that they'll never realize a payback from it. They experience the ripple effect frequently. Some might say they make waves.

Human Ripples

Another kind of ripple is far more important. We produce the ripple by the words we use and the things we do. Sometimes our ripples are positive. Other times they aren't.

We all know people who are chronic complainers. Their negativity pulls others into their foul moods. They're unhappy and try to bring others down to their level of pessimism. In doing so, they have a negative ripple effect. The ripples they generate produce an undertow. We need to guard ourselves around such folks or risk being sucked in and pulled down.

Sadly, some people produce no ripples. They have little effect on others, whether good or bad, positive or negative. I'm not sure how this happens. Surely, at some point, they must have had a ripple effect, but now it's gone. These people aren't much fun to be around, either. There's no movement, no influence, nothing. They inanely move from project to project and from day to day, in rote subsistence. No ripples.

Other people make positive ripples. That's who I want to be. I want to have a positive effect on those around me. I want my ripples to motivate, encourage, and support, to be anticipated and appreciated. We all know people like this too. They're the ones with smiling folks around them, inspiring others to achieve more as they send ripples in all directions for everyone's benefit.

Life Lesson

Today is the day. Let's go make some positive ripples.

GENEROSITY

LOOK FOR WAYS TO HELP OTHERS

I once worked in a downtown office. Homeless people would sometimes interrupt my short trek from my car to the building to ask for money.

Not wanting to get involved, I'd shake my head and say, "I don't have any money on me." Sometimes this was true. Other times, I felt guilty for lying.

I wanted to do better.

Later, I went to an urban church that attracted a lot of homeless and financially marginalized people. They, too, had needs, which they were more than happy to share with me.

Because of these experiences, I determined to

strive to help people who were truly in need, while working even harder to ensure I didn't enable them in their less-than-ideal situations or be taken advantage of.

To achieve this goal, I'd seek to verify their actual need. This required talking to them. It meant listening with discernment. It meant unraveling their web of deceit to find out its root cause. Many times, they'd grow weary of my probing and give up. They'd make an awkward retreat and leave me so they could go find an easier mark.

Other times I'd end up putting myself in an unwise situation—or at least it seemed that way in hindsight. Yet God protected me in my naiveté. Though I'd never give them money, I would buy them things. It might be a burger at a quick-serve restaurant or a bag of groceries. I might purchase a bus pass for them or put gas in their car. Once I even offered to cover a motel room for one night. But when the guy was a no-show, I realized he didn't want a place to sleep as much as the money the room represented.

Despite my careful efforts, in retrospect, I think they conned me more often than not.

Through these experiences, I realized the sure-fire way to make sure no one ever took advantage of my generosity. It's quite simple. Never give, and they'll never take advantage of you.

Given this sobering truth, I persist in being open to help people address their genuine needs, while being a discerning steward of money. I don't have as many opportunities to exercise this anymore, as I now live in a rural area with no visible homelessness and little poverty.

In considering the situation on a larger scale—regional, national, and international—pressing needs continue to confront me. To manage expectations with a clear conscience, I determined areas I would consider. The rest could receive a quick guilt-free decline.

For me, these areas are clean water, microfinance, Bibles, native missionaries, and local organizations I'm personally involved with. I give serious consideration to needs in these areas. Otherwise, the request receives an easy no.

Sometimes my contributions are not monetary. Instead, I give my time or my possessions.

As I'm open to helping people in need and supporting areas I'm passionate about, it's not merely about giving money, time, or resources. It's also the satisfaction of knowing that in my small way I've made the world a bit better.

This is what happens when we freely give.

Life Lesson

We need to help others as often as we can.

RESPECT THE ENVIRONMENT
PURSUE A HEALTHY BALANCE AND AVOID EXTREME RESPONSES

After months of waiting, I headed out for a spiritual retreat. I arrived with anticipation of my time there. Though not enforced with unbending resolve, the center promotes silence. It stands as one of their values. I relished the promise of solitude in their rural, nearly untainted environment.

Filled with expectation, I settled into my preassigned room. After a wordless dinner, enjoyed with my fellow sojourners, I explored the retreat center's many forested paths. I walked about a mile, only covering a portion of the property's crisscrossing trails. Since it was a humid evening, moisture soon formed on my skin and then dripped off my body.

My usual strides embrace intentionality, but

that's not an ideal tempo for spiritual contemplation. Yet when I slowed my gait, the bugs assaulted me. Out of self-preservation, their attacks forced me to maintain a brisk pace, even though I would have preferred to meander in this pristine paradise.

I spotted deer tracks on the path, first one set and then a second. I rounded a bend in the wooded trail and was surprised to see a deer some thirty feet away.

With no antlers, I surmised it was a doe. But as I got closer and could make out details, I assumed it was a fawn, albeit a mature one since it was mid-August. Even though I was unsure if it was a doe or a buck, I persisted in thinking of the deer as female.

She showed no fear. She did not run away.

We just stared at each other. I stood in awe. She seemed curious about me. I wondered if this is what it was like with Adam and Eve in their idyllic Eden paradise.

I had an unexplained urge to talk to the doe, but that would be irrational, so I remained quiet. I was willing to linger in this moment, but the insect portion of creation wanted to feast on my blood, so I eased slowly forward. The deer stood still as I gingerly approached.

I expected my advance would spook her, but she

didn't budge. When I closed to within twenty feet, she leisurely sauntered off the trail. She never ran or showed any sign of fear but ambled off into the woods, seemingly unconcerned with my presence. I circled around and five minutes later found her in about the same spot. She spied me watching her, but nonchalantly returned to sniffing the ground before her.

I covered more trails that evening, communing with God as I walked. That's when I received insight about creation and our mandate to steward it wisely. At creation, God told Adam and Eve to be fruitful and multiply, to fill the earth and subdue it, and to rule over the animals (Genesis 1:28). To subdue means to bring it under control, but this doesn't give us the right to abuse it. And to rule wisely means we must be good caretakers.

Some view the earth as fragile and insist we must protect it, regardless of cost or inconvenience. Others say that creation is resilient and adaptable, able to counteract whatever people do to it.

There on the wooded trail, I realized both perspectives are right—and both are wrong. Our Creator did indeed make the earth resilient and adaptable, able to deal with anything that nature or animals can throw at it. Yet we must take care to not do anything stupid or extreme.

To our discredit, we've "advanced" to a point where our consumption, greed, and blatant disregard for our world is indeed threatening it. We must, instead, be good stewards and wise caretakers —not out of fear but out of respect.

Life Lesson

We must respect the habitat God has gifted to us.

TAKE CARE OF YOURSELF

WE ONLY GET ONE BODY AND WE MUST RESPECT IT

Too many people in our world today pack their lives full of activity. They treat busyness as a badge of accomplishment. They sacrifice to achieve and receive admiration.

In doing so, they neglect their physical well-being. Their body suffers, but they push health aside in their pursuit for more. They reason that modern medicine can provide a pill to counter the side effects of their neglect.

Yet they do this to their peril.

Here are three areas I address to take care of myself, to treat my body as the sacred temple it is.

Exercise

I start my day with exercise. I've done this my entire adult life. Yet I've added to my routine over the years.

I began with an exercise bike, riding for about fifteen minutes a day. Over the years, I've worn out two bikes and am working on a third. Its odometer has turned over twice.

Later, I added a stair stepper to my exercise arsenal. For a time, I did weights, too, but set them aside as being too dreary. Maybe someday I'll return to them.

My last addition is an inversion table. I'm not sure if inverting constitutes exercise, but my back sure appreciates it.

My morning exercise routine also has a spiritual component because I integrate it with prayer and Bible reading.

More recently, I added a midday walk to my exercise regimen. With an aim of fifteen to twenty minutes a day, I often do more, except for when the weather forces me to stay inside.

These efforts may not align with an ideal recommended exercise routine—and are not medical advice to follow—but they are something I can embrace and adhere to. I get my body moving and my heart pumping. That's what matters.

Food

Next up is food. We must eat to live, not live to eat. This is a key perspective. It's important we do not lose sight of this. Food is the means, not the end.

A coworker I once often traveled with remarked about my eating habits. He noted that my breakfasts were both wise and healthy. My lunches were mostly good, while healthy considerations were largely absent from my days' concluding meals.

He was right. My self-discipline decreased throughout the day, and my eating habits reflected this. I've since worked to correct this oversight. Now I strive to eat three healthy meals every day—morning, noon, and night.

I drink a lot of water throughout the day to stay hydrated. For liquids, I consume mostly water and milk, with a healthy glass of apple juice each morning. I minimize soft drinks and caffeine, while I never drink coffee or alcoholic beverages.

Next, I'm working on increasing my intake of fruits and vegetables while decreasing carbs. I'm also striving to move away from my perception that

I need a dessert after every meal. I'm working toward having just one a day and reducing the size of the portion as well.

And I now resist the urge for an evening snack.

I also take a daily dose of vitamin C, vitamin D, and zinc. I also fast one day each week; it has both physical and spiritual benefits.

Again, my eating practices are not recommended health advice. I share them for your consideration and to encourage you to be more intentional about what you consume.

Sleep

My last consideration is sleep. It stands between the end of one day and the start of the next. When we don't get enough rest, it lessens our energy and detracts from our judgment. A good night's sleep is critical if we hope to make the most of each new day.

Here are my sleep practices.

I aim for a consistent bedtime of around 10:00 p.m. each night, on both weekdays and weekends.

I don't set an alarm, but I get up when I'm ready. In the summer months, this happens between 5:00 and 6:00 a.m., whereas for the winter it shifts to between 6:00 and 7:00, as affected by when the sun rises.

This means I get seven to nine hours of sleep each night. Interestingly, I have more energy in the summer than I do in the winter, even though I sleep less.

And one more thing about rest. Because I work at home, if I get tired during the day, I can take a quick nap. Five to ten minutes is all I need to rejuvenate myself and sharpen my focus. This isn't a daily habit, but it seems to occur once or twice each week.

We must be intentional about taking care of our bodies. This includes exercising, eating sensibly, and getting enough rest.

Life Lesson
If we fail to take care of ourselves now, our bodies will fail us later.

BE PRESENT

HONOR PEOPLE BY PRIORITIZING THEM
OVER TECHNOLOGY

M any years ago, back when smartphones first entered the work-force, I attended an industry convention. I sat at a round table with nine others to eat lunch. The keynote address would soon follow.

As each attendee at my table finished eating, they pushed away their plates and pulled out their smartphones. One by one, they gave the device their full attention, as if its contents were all that mattered. Soon, my nine compatriots had their noses buried in their electronic gadgets.

I did not. I sought to be present in the moment. My efforts were in vain, however, because I sat alone with nine others who didn't care about talking or being present. The distant call of non time-sensitive information beckoned.

As the emcee introduced our keynote speaker, I expected them to stow their phones. They did not. Surely, once he began his address, they'd give him their full attention. They did not.

Their companies had sent them there to learn. But they were not fully engaged. In addition, most conference attendees say they learn the most during the informal times between the scheduled speakers. Our lunch would qualify. Yet they missed that opportunity too. And then there's networking, the tertiary benefit of attending conventions. But they weren't attempting that either.

It's as if the convention were a distraction from whatever interesting information their smartphones offered. Though their bodies were present, their minds were distant.

Smartphone preoccupation is epidemic. It has infiltrated work, home, and social settings. At the first hint of idle time, users retrieve their phones and give them their focus. It's also become an acceptable distraction whenever someone becomes bored or in situations when they don't know what to say or do. It stands as an acceptable alternative to being present in the moment and giving people around them their attention.

More recently, I've seen this smartphone distraction occur at sporting events, both at professional contests and at kids' games. For the first, they paid a lot of money to be there. Yet they failed to watch all of it because they let their phones divert their attention. For the latter, I presume they showed up to support their kids. But they didn't. At best, their minds were only partially present, as they diverted their attention to their devices. Their kid made a move worthy of celebration, but they missed it.

Smartphone distraction occurs in other settings too. More than once, I've seen a child check to see if their parents noticed what they just did. Disappointment covered their face when they realized their parents were oblivious to what occurred.

Too often I've heard a child beg, "Watch me, Mommy!" or "Daddy, see what I'm doing!" At best, the parent glanced up, gave an approving nod, and mumbled a halfhearted affirmation as they resumed scrutinizing their phone.

Put your phones away! Be present in the moment. Your kids will grow up fast. They may move away and not have time for you. But that's okay. They learned it from you.

When I got my smartphone, I pledged to not be one of those people. By intention, I have no social media apps on my phone. I only recently installed email on it, which I've only used one time. Seriously. Just once.

I promised myself that when in the company of others, I would only pull out my phone for emergencies. I then added one other use for my phone when I'm with people. It's to check on something relevant to our conversation. Other than that, it stays tucked away.

I want to be present in the moment, fully engaged. I strive to give people my priority and relegate my smartphone to its rightful place, which is out of sight. That's where it belongs and where it will stay, even if I must squirm in awkward silence. That's because people matter so much more than the distractions of posts and pics.

Life Lesson

We must put our smartphones away and strive to be present in every moment.

PURSUE COMMUNITY
DON'T LIVE IN ISOLATION

J ohn Donne said, "No man is an island, entire of itself." We will do well to heed his wise words. Though many people celebrate the rugged individual, individualism is a lonely place to be. We need people. Going it alone isolates. We are emotionally and physically healthier when we connect in community. Our mental health depends on it.

Besides family and neighbors, we should pursue other connections as well. This goes beyond the workplace and extends to the area where we live. Doing so adds value to our life and forms meaningful relationships outside of home and work.

Community Considerations

Here are some areas to pursue:

Nonprofits: Look for worthy nonprofit organizations to support. They don't just need your money. They need your time too. As you give, you'll form meaningful connections with those gathered around a common interest.

Service Groups: Consider service groups and parachurch organizations. These, too, can provide a place to belong, working with others to achieve a shared goal.

Church: The connections enjoyed in a church setting offer psychological benefits as well as spiritual. Don't dismiss church until you try it. Make a focused attempt to connect with other people there.

And if you tried church and found it lacking, don't dismiss the idea. Try it afresh. Keep searching for a place to belong.

Community Essentials

The purpose of pursuing community is to form connections, which has a side effect of enhancing our lives. Yet to realize connections that last, these communities need an outward focus, not an inward selfishness.

Groups that seek only to serve themselves and exclude others crumble in a couple of years. Those with an outward focus can last much longer.

As we connect with others, we'll live a more fulfilling life and benefit society. As a bonus, it's when we seek to connect with others that we receive the most.

Life Lesson

We're not meant to go through life alone. We need others, and they need us. We need community.

～

If you liked *Sticky Living*, please leave a review online. Your review will help others discover this book and encourage them to read it too. Thank you.

～

Do you want to continue the journey of *Sticky Living*? Check out *Bridging the Sacred-Secular Divide*.

OTHER BOOKS IN THE STICKY SERIES

Which book in the Sticky Series do you want to read next?

- **Sticky Customer Service**: Stop Churning Customers and Start Growing Your Business
- **Sticky Sales and Marketing**: Produce Positive Long-Term Results and Relationships
- **Sticky Leadership and Management**: Lead with Integrity and Manage with Confidence

ABOUT PETER LYLE DEHAAN

Peter Lyle DeHaan is an entrepreneur and businessman who has managed, owned, or started multiple businesses over his career. Common themes at every turn have included leadership and management, customer service, and sales and marketing.

He shares his lifetime of business experience and personal insights with others through his books and blog posts to encourage, inspire, and occasionally entertain.

Learn more at peterlyledehaan.com.

BOOKS BY PETER LYLE DEHAAN

Sticky Series

Sticky Customer Service

Sticky Sales and Marketing

Sticky Leadership and Management

Sticky Living

Call Center Success Series

Call Center Connections

Healthcare Call Center Essentials

How to Start a Telephone Answering Service

Other Books

Successful Author FAQs

Academic Research

The Telephone Answering Service Industry

Turning a Telephone Answering Service into a Call Center

For the latest list of all Peter Lyle DeHaan's books, go to peterlyledehaan.com/books/

www.ingramcontent.com/pod-product-compliance
Lightning Source LLC
Chambersburg PA
CBHW071650210326
41597CB00017B/2168